EXERCISE FOR A LONGER LIFE
A Guide for Men Over 40

Jonathan P. Brazee

Semper Fi Press

Graphic Design by Worawoot Sittivej

NOTES

This book is targeted for men over 40 who want to get back into shape. While the information presented here certainly pertains to women and men under 40, some of the points take into account the issues experienced as men get older, especially those who have not been in a rigorous exercise regimen.

       The book is broken into three parts. The first part is a summary of some of the thousands of studies that have examined the effects of exercise on human longevity. This is to highlight the need for everyone to exercise,

       The second part covers some of the considerations that should be taken into account before starting an exercise regimen. It is never too late to begin, but going about it incorrectly can do more harm than good.

       The third part of the book is the appendices where samples are provided of both specific exercises, routines, and log-keeping.

       This book focuses on exercise with the goal to increase both the length of life as well as the quality of life. While the information presented can assist in all aspects of exercise, it is not intended to create bodybuilders, endurance athletes, or any other type of high fitness lifestyles, nor is in targeted to those who already have an active exercise regimen.

TABLE OF CONTENTS

Exercise and live better.

Exercise and live longer.

Science has long understood the relationship between fitness and life expectancy. People who are fit live longer than those who are not. This is common sense, but there has been the chicken and egg question: do people who are fit live longer and healthier, or is it that people who are healthier are more likely to exercise and keep fit? In other words, can someone increase his or her life expectancy and life quality by exercise, or is it those who are naturally healthy and longer-lived are more apt to feel up to an exercise routine?

Recent studies, though, conducted around the world, have shown conclusively that it is the exercise, and more specifically the strength achieved through exercise, that makes people live longer and healthier. Even after correcting for potential cofounders such as cardiorespiratory fitness and lifestyle choices such as smoking and diet, the results were pretty clear that both muscular and aerobic fitness result in a lower incidence of death from all causes, from cancer to cardiac disease to accidents.

It is not just a longer life, though, that is the result of exercise, but a richer life. People who exercise regularly have sex more often and find it more gratifying. People who exercise are more mobile, can take care of themselves better, and suffer fewer mental problems such as depression and Alzheimer's.

However, and this is a big however, the human body does age. Someone who is 60 years old does not have the same body as when he was 20, and too much exercise, or more accurately, exercise done incorrectly, can have adverse effects on the body. And exercise regimen for a 20-year-old is probably not appropriate for a 60-year-old and even less appropriate for an 80-year-old. Exercise is probably even more vital for the older man, but it needs to be adjusted to provide the most benefit without damage or injury.

This guide will briefly look at the science of both exercise and aging, then provide advice and guidance on how an older person can create his own exercise regimen in order to maximize his overall health, happiness, and long life.

<u>SENESCENSE (AGING)</u>

Senescence, or aging, is a fact of life, something no one can escape other than by death. As we age, our bodies change, and those changes can and will have a major impact on our lives.

Gerontology is the science that studies the aging process to prevent age-related disease and degeneration, preserve health, and prolong human life. Senescence is the process of aging, while in the context of this guide, exercise is one of the methods, discovered through gerontology, that combats the effects of aging.

So what exactly is aging? The long and short of it is that we don't exactly know. We can observe the results, but as for the causation, that is still somewhat of a mystery. With each new advance and discovery in molecular or cellular biology, new theories spring up. Currently, most theories center around what are termed damage-based theories and programmed theories.

Damaged-based theories are based on the concept that aging results from a continuous process of damage accumulation originating in by-products of metabolism; that is, damage accumulates throughout a person's entire lifespan, and that causes aging. Usually, this damage is a by-product of normal cellular processes or a consequence of inefficient repair systems.

Programmed theories of aging contend that aging is not a result of random processes but rather a genetic-based. Our cells have "clocks" that turn them off at certain times in our lives.

While science does not have a consensus on just what causes aging, the effects are far more evident. Aging can be defined as a progressive functional decline or a gradual deterioration of physiological function with age. Humans, as they age, become more susceptible to disease and death. Our ability to function as biological organisms decline. This is pretty self-evident. Most of us have either experienced this type of decline or witnessed it in others.

The process of aging is generally accepted as starting after the sexual peak, normally at about 19 years of age for men. In brief, aging is characterized by a lower metabolic rate, changes in appearance such as a gradual reduction in height and weight loss due to loss of muscle and bone mass and compression of the spinal discs, longer reaction times, declines in certain memory functions, a decline in frequency of sexual activity, a decline in hearing, the sense of smell, and vision, declines in pulmonary, kidney, and cardio functions, declines in exercise performance, and multiple endocrinal changes. Although the immune system deteriorates with age, called immunosenescence, a major hallmark of aging is an increase in inflammation levels that may contribute to several age-related disorders such as Alzheimer's disease, atherosclerosis and arthritis. Some age-related changes, such as farsightedness, which appears to be a universal trait of human aging, and menopause, which affects women, are inevitable, yet the how and when these age-related declines occur can vary considerably between specific individuals.[1]

Let's examine some of the specific aspects of aging, aspects that can be combated by increased fitness levels. The first is the degradation of the body's mitochondria.

Mitochondria are known as the powerhouses of the cell. They are organelles that act as a digestive system that takes in nutrients, breaks them down, and creates energy for the cell. This process is known as cellular respiration. Most of the chemical reactions involved in cellular respiration happen in the mitochondria.

One cell could have several thousand mitochondria. The number depends on what the cell needs to do. If the purpose of the cell is to transmit nerve impulses, there will be fewer mitochondria than in a muscle cell which require much more energy to function. As we age, our mitochondria start to degrade, resulting in weaker cells and muscle fibers. We experience this as decreased levels of endurance, strength, and function.

An enzyme that has a significant effect on aging is telomerase. Our bodies grow and renew through the process of mitosis, which is when a "parent cell" divides into two "daughter" cells. During mitosis, cells make copies of their genetic material. Half of the genetic material goes to each new daughter cell. To make sure that information is successfully passed from one generation to the next, each chromosome has a special protective cap called a telomere located at the end of its "arms." Telomeres are controlled by the presence telomerase. When telomerase is degraded, so is the ability for the body to maintain vitality through the cell renewal of mitosis.

Osteoporosis is a progressive bone disease characterized by a decrease in bone mass and density which can lead to an increased risk of fractures and ability to maintain posture. The bone mineral density is reduced, bone microarchitecture

Jonathan P. Brazee

deteriorates, and the amount and variety of proteins in bone are altered. Osteoporosis is not just a disease of women, as is sometimes thought, but can also affect men.

Cognitive ability becomes compromised. Alzheimer's Disease is perhaps the most widely discussed form of cognitive disorder, but simple senility, or "senior moments," affect the ability to think things through or to remember even simple tasks.

Finally, the body starts to produce less and less testosterone. With less of the hormone, we lose muscle and bone mass as well as sexual functionality. Low testosterone also affects the production of red blood cells, fat distribution and can lead to depression and other mental issues.

There are many more effects related to aging, of course, but these are just a few of the effects that will be addressed in this guide.

EXERCISE AND AGING

We exercise for a number of reasons. It improves our health, makes us better able to conduct daily tasks, makes us feel better about ourselves, giving us confidence, and reduces stress and anxiety. For some of us, it is also an opportunity for socialization, whether that is group interaction such as with the Hash House Harriers or merely informal chatting at the gym with other gym-goers.

One very important fact that has been revealed, though, is that exercise, in particular resistance weight-training, has a very significant effect on longevity. With numerous scientifically valid studies, all of them showed varying degrees of increasing the life span as a result of exercise. A general median is that a moderate exercise regimen can increase the life span by about six to seven years. Not only does it increase the life span, but it increases the quality of life during those years.

The British Journal of Medicine published the results of an analysis of 30 comprehensive studies that is considered a milestone on the issue of fitness and longevity. The results were pretty conclusive. The studies recorded physical attributes such as bench press strength, grip strength, walking speed, chair rising speed, and standing balance. What the researchers found was that poor performance on any of the tests was associated with higher all-cause mortality, anywhere from a 1.67 to a threefold increase in the likelihood of earlier mortality.

With the current body or research, there is little scientific doubt that exercise increases the life span. The key is to do the correct exercise regimen for each individual.

How Does Exercise Increase Life Span?

As mentioned earlier, science does not even understand how aging works, so a firm response to the question cannot be given. However, there are some indications that seem to hold water.

Mitochondrial degradation is a primary culprit in dwindling muscle mass. Recent evidence, though, indicates that exercise can slow down this effect. According to Mark Tarnopolsky, a professor of pediatrics and medicine at McMaster University in Hamilton, Ontario, resistance training activates a muscle stem cell called a satellite cell. In what is known as "gene shifting," these new cells cause the mitochondria to rejuvenate. Tarnopolsky claims that after six months of twice weekly strength exercise training, the biochemical, physiological, and genetic signature of older muscles are "turned back" by a factor of 15 to 20 years.

Studies involving middle-aged athletes indicate that high intensity exercise protects people at the chromosomal level as well. It appears that exercise stimulates the production of telomerase, what allows for the ongoing maintenance of genetic information and cellular integrity. Exercise also triggers the production of antioxidants, which boosts the health of the body in general.

Other studies are successfully linking athleticism to longevity. A recent analysis of a study conducted in Germany revealed that more than 900,000 athletes (ranging in age from 20 to 79) showed no significant age-related decline in performance appeared before the age of 55. Even beyond that age, the decline was surprisingly slow: in the 65 to 69 group, a quarter of the athletes performed above the average among the 20 to 54 year-old group.

Essentially, exercise helps the body regenerate itself. This likely explains why older athletes are less susceptible to age-related illnesses than their sedentary counterparts. Moreover, steady exercise has been shown to lessen lean tissue loss. It also helps to maintain strength and mobility, which can significantly reduce risk of injury and stave off health problems that would otherwise linger.

Even more remarkable is how resistance training can stave off cognitive decline — what is arguably just as important as physical well-being. In a study conducted at the University of British Columbia, women between the ages of 70 and 80 who were experiencing mild cognitive impairment were put through 60-minute classes two times per week for 26 weeks. They used a pressurized air system (for resistance) and free weights and were told to perform various sets of exercises with variable loads. The results were significant: lifting weights improved memory and helped stave off the effects of dementia. It also improved the seniors' attention span and ability to resolve conflicts.

The conclusion for this study was that researchers believe that resistance training done twice a week could serve as a promising strategy to stave off the effects of cognitive decline in seniors, especially the onset of Alzheimer's. It's also clear from the study that, when supervised and guided properly, seniors can reap the physical benefits of weight training as well.[2]

The above studies focuses on weight training, but straight cardio training has also shown to be as beneficial to increasing the lifespan. The most famous study is perhaps the Copenhagen City study, which monitored over 20,000 men and women aged from 20 to 90. Within this number were 1,116 male and 762 female joggers. The health history between the joggers and non-joggers were detailed, and the joggers had a far lower mortality rate than the non-joggers. The adjusted increase in life expectancy for men was 6.2 years and women 5.6 years, surprisingly close to what was observed in studies on weight-lifters.[3]

An ancillary benefit of both forms of exercise is one that has a tremendous effect on longevity: weight loss. Obesity is a major cause of early death in the world. In the US alone, over 120,000 people die each year from preventable obesity-related causes. Cardio and resistance training work to fight obesity in different ways, but both are effective.

Cardio training burns calories through exertion. This keeps the body leaner. Leaner is generally healthier. A good cardio regimen also maintains a higher metabolism. Resistance training, on the other hand, while it does burn up calories through exertion, also relies on building up muscle mass. More muscle means more calories burnt even while at rest. The amount of energy needed to fuel the body is greater, so more calories are burnt rather than being stored as fat.

Exercise also delivers other health benefits. It improves oxygen uptake, increases insulin sensitivity, improves lipid profiles (raising HDL and lowering triglycerides), lowers blood pressure, reduces platelet aggregation, increases fibrinolytic activity, improves cardiac function, bone density, immune function, reduces inflammation markers, and improves psychological function.

Cardio vs. Weight Training

Cardio is a form of aerobic training. "Aerobic" means "with oxygen" and refers to the increased intake of oxygen required for the exercise. Weight training, or resistance training, is anaerobic, and it builds strength and muscle mass.

Frequent and regular aerobic exercise has been shown to help prevent or treat serious and life-threatening chronic conditions such as high blood pressure, obesity, heart disease,

Type 2 diabetes, insomnia, and depression. Weight training appears to have continuous energy-burning effects that persist for about 24 hours after the training, though they do not offer the same cardiovascular benefits of aerobic exercises. Both aerobic and anaerobic exercise also work to increase the mechanical efficiency of the heart by increasing cardiac volume (aerobic exercise), or myocardial thickness (anaerobic training).

According to the European Food Information Council, aerobics notably does not increase the basal metabolic rate as much as some forms of weight training and may therefore be less effective at reducing obesity. However, this form of exercise also allows for longer, more frequent activity and consumes more energy when the individual is active. In addition, the metabolic activity of an individual is heightened for several hours following a bout of aerobic activity.

Any exercise is good, and a combination of cardio and resistance training is optimal. However, there are a few differences with regards to each training option.

The health benefits of cardio training are maximized by moderate training, the so-called "Goldilocks Zone." Dr. James O'Keefe, a research cardiologist and a former elite athlete, coined the term that for health and longevity, it is "The Survival of the Moderately Fit." According to him, "Darwin was wrong about one thing. It's not survival of the fittest, but survival of the moderately fit. Further attainments of peak fitness do not translate into further increases in life expectancy. It plateaus out. We weren't born to run. We were born to walk, and we need to be walking more. . . you need to be moving your body more than sitting: every chance you get, move! " [4]

Research has indicated that about 40 minutes of moderate cardio three times a week maximizes the benefits. Longer than that adds no additional benefit, and much more can actually damage the heart and circulatory system. Extended extreme cardio sets in motion inflammatory mechanisms that can damage the heart, and veteran endurance athletes have five times the risk of atrial and ventricular fibrillation, the latter which can lead to sudden heart death.

On the other hand, resistance training has no such known serious potential. The risk to resistance training is primarily of injury, particularly to older people. This can be serious in its own right and can put a halt to exercise, but they are not particularly life-threatening.

This is not meant to imply that one or the other should be ignored. The best exercise regimen makes use of both cardio and resistance training.

Strength or Muscle Mass?

Sarcopenia (muscle mass) mass is a strong indicator when determining the prospective life span of a given individual. This is an accepted scientific fact. However, the question has arisen if it is simple muscle mass or strength that is a better precursor.

Of course, people with a higher percentage of muscle mass tend to be stronger. Generally, large muscles are stronger than small muscles. However, that is not something set in stone as a geometric progression. Body builders, for example, are usually not as strong as competition weight lifters of a given weight class despite having a higher percentage of muscle mass.

One study, published in the Journal of Gerontology, seems to indicate that it is not muscle mass, per se, that is the best indicator for longevity, but rather that actual strength of the individual.

If this study holds true, then it might be better to design an exercise regimen that emphasizes strength training rather than body building. I should stress, however, that the results in the journal are indicative but need to be repeated in many more studies to be accepted as fact.[5]

Sex

As mentioned above, aging is often accompanied by a reduced production of testosterone, and accompanied with circulatory and possible self-esteem issues, a lack of sexual drive or performance issues. Many of these issues can be alleviated through exercise.

It is commonly accepted that the most important sex organ is the brain. If a person does not feel sexy, he or she will not feel the same degree of sexual interest. Exercise is one method to increase a person's self-esteem. Whether that is a matter of simply losing weight or building up a set of "guns" that attract a potential partner, a degree of self-confidence can do wonders for a sex drive. This may seem to be self-evident, but people who exercise have an improved body image over people who do not exercise. Being more comfortable with your body leads to better and more relaxed sex. One study showed that more physically fit men and women rated their own sexual desirability higher than less active men and women the same age. Eighty percent of men and 60% of females who exercised two to three times weekly rated their own sexual desirability as above average. As the number of days of exercise per week increased, so did the ratings of sexual desirability. Another study showed that men and women who were more physically fit rated their own sexual performance higher. Among people who exercised four to five days per week, 88% of the women and 69% of the men reported their own sexual performance as above average or much above average. The reason for this could simply be an increase in confidence because of an improved body image, or a physiological reason (such as better circulation and blood flow).

The bottom line is that people who exercise more have more sex. This can be because of a better overall physical fitness level that enables a person to be more physically active in bed or it could be because of the psychological reasons identified above, but the results of every study show that the frequency of sex was higher for those who exercise than among those who did not exercise.

This does not change as people get older. Sixty-year-olds who exercise frequently report having the same amount of sex and sexual pleasure as people decades younger. One study examined the sexual frequency and satisfaction ratings of swimmers aged 60 and found that they were the same as those 20 years younger.

There are probably a number of reasons for the increase in sexual activity from a physiological standpoint. One is the increase of testosterone as mentioned above. Another is that people who exercise produce more endorphins, the "feel good" hormones that are released into the bloodstream upon activities such as sex and exercise. The famed "runners' high" is an example of this. Whether caused by exercise or sex, an increased production of endorphins makes it easier to produce them the next time. That includes easier production during sex, and that makes it more pleasurable.

Erectile dysfunction is a problem afflicting many men, especially as they get older. There is the saying that "penis health is heart health." The penis needs a good blood flow to achieve an erection, and problems such as high blood pressure, blocked arteries, and cardiovascular issues can lead to ED. While not a cure-all for all causes of ED, all of these issues can be positively affected by exercise. Researchers looked at men over the age of 50 and found that those who were physically active reported better erections and a 30% lower risk of impotence than men who were inactive.

Age and Exercise

Part of the problem with exercise for older people is that starting or maintaining a regular exercise routine can seem to be an undaunted. It can just seem too much when beset by illness, ongoing health problems, of fear of injury.

While these may seem like good reasons to slow down and take it easy as you age, they're actually even better reasons to get going with an exercise regimen. As delineated above, exercise can energize your mood, relieve stress, help you manage symptoms of illness and pain, and improve your overall sense of well-being. Exercise can be the answer to the very problems that might make you hesitant to get going.

No matter your age or your current physical condition, you can benefit from exercise. One important fact to remember is that it is never too late in life to start exercising. Elderly study subjects showed the positive effects of gene shifting—even when they had never lifted weight before. The key is in designing a regimen that maximizes benefits while minimizing the chance for injury or harm to the body.

As the body ages, in addition to the issues already mentioned, it basically breaks down. Bones lose density, tendons lose strength, joints get arthritic, and a lifetime of injuries and wear and tear start to take their toll. Lean body mass decreases, caused in part by loss of muscle tissue (atrophy). Lipofuscin (an age-related pigment) and fat are deposited in muscle tissue. The muscle fibers shrink. Muscle tissue is replaced more slowly, and lost muscle tissue may be replaced with a tough fibrous tissue. This is most noticeable in the hands, which may appear thin and bony. Changes in the muscle tissue, combined with normal aging changes in the nervous system, cause muscles to have less tone and ability to contract. Muscles may become rigid with age and may lose tone. Osteoarthritis affects one out of two people over the age of 60. This can make any movement, much less exercise, uncomfortable or even painful.

None of this is an excuse though. Everyone can begin a regimen appropriate for his or her physical condition.

After a career in the Marines, my own body is pretty beat up. I am missing a part of my right shoulder courtesy of my tour in Iraq. I have an arthritic wrist thanks to a parachute accident, and my right knee is shot thanks to sports and running. I cannot run much now, nor can I lift my right arm much above shoulder level. However, while I can't do incline presses (or declines) with a barbell, I can still do a straight press, and I can bench in the top 5% of men—not for my age group, but for all men. In my age group, I am in the top 2%.

But my case is nothing. When I was at the Pentagon, my workout partner was a Marine who had one arm shot off when his helicopter was shot down. He would unscrew his "social arm" and put on a metal claw to exercise. When I was going to therapy for my shoulder at Camp Pendleton, there were Marines and sailors who had lost limbs, who were terribly burnt, who were blinded, and nothing would keep them out of the gym.

The bottom line is that all of us, if we live long enough, will have physical problems. Those problems cannot be used as an excuse not to exercise. We just have to have the discipline to buckle down and do it. Many of our aches and pains can be alleviated through exercise, but even if they can't, the exercise will help you in other areas.

EXERCISE FOR THE OLDER MAN

The vital importance of exercise to both longevity and quality of life cannot be overstated. However, an uninformed dive into a strenuous exercise regimen can actually do more harm than good, especially as a man ages. It is important to exercise, but that exercise should be conducted smartly.

This guide is not intended to be a complete exercise encyclopedia. This is a guide in order to point out some considerations, then point the reader in the right direction to create an individually-tailored exercise regimen.

One important point is that people are not the same. This guide is intended for the moderately healthy individual who wants to begin a lifestyle change, and the guidance is targeted for the average older man. If you have any underlying physical condition, if you are morbidly obese, or if you have any other underlying factors, please see a physician before you commence your program.

Rules for Exercise

No rules are all-encompassing for all people. However, the following are a good starting point for most middle-age to elderly men.

- o   No pain means . . . no pain.
- o   Warm up before exercise.
- o   Moderate exercise only.
- o   Exercise two to three times per week.
- o   Form over substance.

No Pain Means . . . No Pain

Of course, the commonly told phrase is "no pain, no gain." For elite athletes, and even for good weekend athletes who are younger, there is some truth in that. However, for the older man, pain is something to avoid.

Pain is nature's way of telling you to stop whatever you are doing. It means let go of the hot frying pan, get out of the blazing sun, take the thorn out of your hand. Pain has evolved over millions of years to be our warning system.

When pain is removed, consequences can be deadly. The fingerless leper is not fingerless because the virus caused the fingers to fall off. The fingers are gone because the leper feels no pain, so all the little cuts and bruises slowly whittle the fingers away.

Nothing is different in the gym. If you pull a muscle while lifting, the pain you feel is telling you to stop. So stop!

In our society, we are taught that real men push through pain. We won't let pain slow us down. That is bad enough for the young ball-player, but as we age, our ability to heal is compromised. It takes longer for us to heal from injury. What might stop us from training for a week when we are 20 might mean a month or more off from training if we receive that same injury when we are 60. A month off for a 60-year-old can set him back to square one as far as keeping up his fitness.

When my shoulder kept me from my preferred sports and I had to exercise in the gym instead, I found my biceps were developing well. Going through a divorce, I will readily admit that I rather liked the attention women were giving my biceps. It was a huge ego boost for them to wrap their hands around them while I flexed. I started curling heavier and heavier dumbbells, forgoing form just to get the weights up. When my bicipital tendons started to complain, I ignored the pain and pushed through it, all to get those guns. Finally, though, my elbows rebelled. I simply could not use my arms in a flexed position for anything, even to carry in groceries in the crook of my arm. I saw a doctor, and he told me to stop my curls.

Three years later, and with my biceps much smaller, I finally started to curl again, albeit at a much lower weight. And if I feel the twinge of pain in my elbows when I do the reps, I immediately stop and go on to something else.

I let my ego get in the way of common sense. As a result, I lost three years of adductive training for my upper arms.

Painless exercise does not mean effortless exercise, though. Exercise is useless unless there is work involved. Your muscles should feel fatigue. You should be breathing hard, and your pulse rate should be up. However, a sharp, knifing pain cannot be ignored, and whatever is causing that pain should be stopped, and if the pain persists, should initiate a visit to a doctor.

Warm up Before Exercise

One of the most common mistakes I see at the gym is for people to come in, sit on a machine or free weight station, and commence vigorous exercise. When the resistance is low, this can be done, but even then, it is not a good idea. Exercising without a proper warm up elevates the risk of injury, and injury is the older man's Waterloo.

Even when warming up, a poor methodology can actually damage the body even more than with no warm up at all. A very common mistake is for someone to rush into a few jumping jacks, then "bounce" stretch, that is, use momentum to get the body past points of stiffness. This is a major error. This is a form of static stretching that can tear open the tiny repairs in the muscle that occurs during your last workout (more to come later on that).

Many physical trainers now recommend that static stretching, at least for weightlifting, not be done at all. However, according to the American College of Sports Medicine, it is still a good idea. The ACSM recommends stretching each of the major muscle groups at least two times a week for 60 seconds per exercise. The key point in static stretching is, once again, no pain (are you seeing a pattern here?) Whether the trainers are correct or the ACSM is correct, proper technique is probably good for you at best and shouldn't do any harm at worse.

Dynamic stretching is probably a better way to prepare for the more strenuous part of the day's routine. Dynamic stretching covers a wider range of motion, so the muscles, ligaments, and tendons are "warmed up" through a more natural range of movement. One way to do this is to actually conduct the bench press, leg press, curl, or whatever, but with a minimal weight. If your first set is with the bench press, before adding any weight, simply lift the empty bar, going through the entire range of motion.

Don't limit your stretching to just the gym. Staying flexible is extremely important as a person ages. Yoga and Tai Chi are two exercise options that stress keeping flexible. You can stretch at home, at work, pretty much anywhere. And while serious exercise should be limited in the number of times per week it is done, stretching can be done daily.

Finally, there is stretching after the workout. I almost hesitate to include this, but if you start going to the gym regularly, you will be faced with it, and you need to understand the pros and cons. There is a movement among some serious weight-lifters to avoid cold stretching, but immediately following the workout, go through some deep stretches, The theory is that that this form of stretching can actually increase the rate of hypertrophy through the increased activation of satellite cells and the enhanced release of growth factors (hepatocyte growth factor, myogenin, IGF-1) within muscle tissue. Research seems to support this, but this type of deep stretching requires that you push beyond the initiation of pain. I just think this is too dangerous for the older man, especially someone fairly new to the gym. The chance of injury is just too great, especially as most weight-lifters who do this use a partner to help push them. That partner cannot feel the pain points, so it is possible that he could actually force you into injury.

My recommendation is to skip the post-workout deep stretch, but that is a choice for you to make on your own. You are the final arbiter of your own body.

Moderate Exercise Only

I cannot stress enough that exercise should be moderate in nature. Research is very clear that beyond a certain point, there is no health benefit to extreme endurance exercise. Quite the opposite, endurance athletes actually have more health problems and die at an earlier age. For resistance training, there may not be the inflammatory results of long distance runners or swimmers, but there is a much greater risk of injury and joint degradation as the weight load increases. Moderate exercise maximizes the health benefits while keeping the risk of injury reasonable.

Once again, though, moderate does not mean effortless. Sitting there doing 10 curls with two-pound dumbbells is not doing you any good. You need to put out the effort for any benefits. You should feel fatigued. You should feel tired. What you should not feel is pain.

Just what is moderation, though? One method taught to the elderly is the talk/sing test. If you cannot talk while or immediately following exercise, if you have to catch your breath first, then you are probably exercising too hard. If you can sing a song during or afterwards, you are probably not exercising hard enough. However, if you can talk, even if somewhat winded, that is probably within the range you want to be.

This, of course, is not an exact test. For younger, generally fit men, it might be a little too lenient. But for obese men of any age and for men 50 years and on up, it is a pretty good off-the-cuff measuring stick.

For lifting weights, moderation is more tied to repetitions and sets. Lifting too heavy puts more stress on joints and connective tissue, and one very heavy lift does not do the body nearly enough good to increase muscle mass. Lifting too light means many, many more repetitions to get any degree of work done. That can also be rough on the joints.

I will go into a little more detail later, but there are basically two different lifting formulas: lifting to failure and lifting by sets. Lifting to failure is lifting a weight until you cannot lift it anymore. Lifting by sets is lifting a given weight X number of times (although that weight can change for each rep).

Regardless of the method, a normal routine would be four sets of a given exercise. When lifting to failure, I try to lift a weight that I can lift 20 times for the first set, then go down from there for the next three sets. This is not standard weight-lifting theory. Most people would recommend lifting a heavier weight fewer times. However, I am very conscious of the strain on my joints, and while I can lift heavier, I don't like the pressure on my joints.

For lifting by sets, most trainers recommend four sets of between eight and twelve reps each. You should be able to lift the full reps for all four sets. If you cannot do the reps for the last set, for example, lower the weight for the next workout.

Exercise Two or Three Times Per Week

Each time you exercise, be it resistance training or cardio, your muscles suffer tiny micro-tears. It is these tears that causes the body to bulk up from exercise. As the body heals them, a little more tissue is created. However, these tears are like any other injury to the body. They need to heal, and that takes time.

Because of this, you should exercise only from two to three times per week. This allows the body time to heal and prepare for the next workout. Furthermore, you should alternate your workout routines. If one day is your heavy day on the weights, the next day should be your light day.

Some people, though, just want to get to the gym more often. This is OK, but only with better management. If Monday is a weight training day, and you want to exercise on Tuesday, then Tuesday should be a cardio day, such as a stationary bike or stair-stepper.   Do not lift weights two days in a row, and do not do significant cardio two days in a row. If you feel the need to exercise four, five, or six days a week, alternate what you do on each of those days.

However, there is no need for exercising that often. Even as little as one session of 40 minutes a week has been shown to increase lifespan.

Form Over Substance

With resistance training, how you do the exercise is more important than how much resistance you are actually working. Yes, you need enough resistance to cause the muscles to exert, but improper form diminishes the value of the repetition and can have serious consequences.

While working out at a local Air Force gym, I sometimes watch people do the CrossFit training. As designed, this is a good system for overall fitness, but without expert guidance, I think it could do more harm than good. As people move from station to station, their form is nowhere near what it should be as they struggle to complete each exercise quickly. Weights are lifted herky-jerky with the body writhing around to get the exercise finished. This is an open invitation to injury. I am not criticizing CrossFit here because with proper trainers, none of this would be allowed. But when people see something, then try it for themselves and use time or weight as a standard, things can go downhill fast.

As I have stressed, pain is the indicator for injury, and injury is the enemy. Lifting weights improperly with poor form just begs for injury. It is far better to lift with excellent form, even with lower weights, and get the benefit of the exercise with the least risk of injury. In a recent *New York Times* article, it was reported that 14% of all weightlifting injuries that required hospitalization were because the weights were too heavy. Heavy weights can put in increased strain on the body, and they tend to degrade the proper form. An improper squat with a light weight might not mean much other than wasting the effort, but the same improper form with a heavy weight could result in serious injury.

Every lift has a proper form. Generally, that means the back straight and the pelvis in. In almost every gym, there are posters on the walls showing the proper form for each exercise. Follow them!

Slow and steady lifts are much, much better than jerks. Lifting within yourself is vital. Paying attention to your posture and the entirety of the motion can keep you on form. Concentrate on each and every aspect.

Good form is not only to reduce the risk of injury. It is also how to maximize results. Slowly lifting increases muscle strength. The correct form concentrates on the muscles you are trying to exercise. I recently watched a man doing crunches with a 25 pound weight behind his head. The problem was that the weight was way too heavy for him, and his "exercise" was only for his neck and possibly his forearms. His abdomen never got through the motion he intended. Good negatives (the act of getting back into the starting position) are also very important.

One last point is that form starts from taking the weight off the rack until you re-rack it after you are finished. It does no good if you bench four sets with perfect form, but when you take the plates off the bar, you simply grab them and go. That is still a 45 pound weight, and without proper form, that is enough to throw your back out.

Common Mistakes and Miscomprehensions

There is a new book out on aging and exercise called *Old School, New Body*. I rather like the list of five mistakes many people make, and as it matches what I am writing here, I will quote it directly:

> **1. Stop The Diets!** Stop eating those low-fat foods that keep being advertised as "healthy" for you. Your body *needs* fat in order to run correctly! Healthy fats are necessary to regenerate your power hormones! For example, testosterone -the strength hormone- is a direct result of cholesterol and dietary fat intake! You need these fats and cholesterol to make all of your hormones so it is important not to cut all of them completely out of your diet! Also, if you're constantly counting all those calories and eating only

low fat, you cannot enjoy eating out! Worrying yourself to death will definitely not make you look younger.

2. Quit your crazy long cardio workouts! – Cardiovascular conditioning can be achieved in far less time and with less effort than those long gym classes and hours on the treadmill. In fact, running on the treadmill and other long bouts of cardio workouts can actually accelerate the aging process by increasing free radicals in your body and there are far smarter ways to exercise. **Free radicals** are like robbers that are deficient in energy. They attack and snatch energy from the other cells to satisfy themselves. Exercise releases free radicals, but when you exercise for a short amount of time, a smaller amount are released and the body can take care of them and prevent damage. But when you do long, extended workouts, free radical damage is out of control which speeds up the aging process!

3. Stop blaming everything on your age! Studies have shown that even people in their 90s have been able to gain muscle tone in less than a month with some lifting exercises. People can change their bodies at any age, from 25 to 95! You should constantly challenge yourself because it's the challenge and the constant work towards improvement that keeps you young! And what better challenge is there than staying fit and healthy?

4. Drink More Water! Water not only hydrates you and keeps you healthy-it also helps to **burn fat!** Water suppresses hunger and keeps your liver and kidneys healthy. Just drinking a dozen ounces a day will drop years from your face by keeping your skin hydrated and healthy! Fun fact: Your liver is the number one fat-burning organ. When you are not drinking enough water, your kidneys stop working and your liver takes over. Do you really want your liver processing water instead of burning fat? Of course not! So start drinking and keep drinking that water to keep everything in your body functioning as it should!

5. Work out LESS! Steve and Becky are not saying to stop working out. They are just saying that you should go by the **old-school resistance training** instead of the hours upon hours of cardio classes like spinning and kickboxing. This resistance-training program includes just four specific exercises that will have you done with your workout while others at the gym are just warming up.[6]

This basically coincides with what current research indicates and falls in line with what I am pushing here.

DIET

No guide on exercise can ignore diet. This guide is not intended to offer extensive diet theory or tell you what to eat. There are plenty of guides, books, websites, and commercial enterprises out there which can offer every type of diet under the sun. But we will touch on a few points here.

When people hear the word "diet," most conjure up images of the obese. Certainly being obese is a serious health risk and a very good reason to begin a serious exercise regimen. But the word diet really has no positive or negative connotation in the true meaning. All it means is what you eat, period. At the base level, a person can have a healthy diet for himself of an unhealthy one.

We are all bombarded with diets to lose weight, from Jenny Craig to the Caveman Diet to the Zone Diet. Less commonly discussed, though, is how an unhealthy diet can be a result of eating disorders. Yes, conditions such as bulimia and anorexia are well documented, but somehow, in our society, we consider those who suffer from those to be "sick" while the obese are considered to be somehow more culpable for their condition.

A poor diet can have drastic consequences to a person's health and well-being. Being overweight AND underweight can take years off a person's lifespan. Being severely underweight had shown to be even more dangerous than being overweight. A sufferer from anorexia and bulimia has a shorter expected lifespan than even the morbidly obese. The body just does not get the proper nutrients to function effectively.

That point needs to be remembered. The body is a machine, and it needs to be fueled. When you exercise, your body needs more fuel and more of the right kinds of fuel. Without the right kinds of fuel, your body may not be able to perform as you want it to.

Calories and Weight

The inarguable formula for weight is calories in versus calories out. If you consume more calories than you burn, you will gain weight. If you consume fewer calories than you consume, you will lose weight. Period.

There are various factors, though, that can affect both the absorption of calories as well as the burning of them. The prime governor of how fast the body burns calories is the metabolic rate of the body. When exercising, that rate goes up. More calories are burned in order to perform the needed work. However, how the body burns calories at rest is also a factor. If you increase the muscle mass of the body, that mass takes far more energy to simply exist than the very low caloric consumption required to keep and equal mass of fat to simply exist. "Trading off" fat for muscle makes the body burn more calories even when at rest.

One problem with many diets, especially the fad or crash diets, is that they drastically reduce the amount of calories taken in. The body realizes this. It knows that it is burning up more calories than it is getting, and it "wants" to maintain an equilibrium. Its solution? Lower the metabolism. If a specific adult male has a "programmed" metabolism that burns 2,600 calories per day, and that man starts a 1,000 calorie a day diet, then his body will try to re-program itself to function at a lower metabolic rate. It can slow down to 2,000 calories, 1,500 calories, even possibly to 1,000 calories per day. This is why many people find great success in the first weeks of a crash diet, but then as the body adjusts, the weight loss stops.

In order for any diet to work, the metabolic rate must remain normal. There are a number of drugs that artificially force the body into a higher rate. Many of these are banned because of the significant increase in risk of death. Usually, these are related to damage the drugs can cause the heart. Exercise, though, is a safe and effective method to maintain the metabolic rate. It is as if the body knows it is not getting enough calories for the work being demanded of it, but it knows it must be able to function, so it goes to the "bank" for more energy. The bank is the fat cells which are storing energy for use.

Every person has his own metabolic rate, every person reacts differently to exercise and diets. It is much more difficult for some people to lose or gain weight than for others, but the bottom line is and always will boil down to calories in versus calories out.

Exercise and Diet

(Here, when I refer to "diet," I am referring to what a person eats, not any specific weight gain or loss formula.)

As noted above, the body needs fuel to function. A healthy exercise regimen needs more fuel than sitting on the couch watching tv. Therefore, it is imperative to fuel the body properly. The human body is designed to function with all of the six components of nutrition:

- o Proteins are involved in growth, repair and general maintenance of the body.

- o Carbohydrates are usually the main energy source for the body.

- o Lipids or fats are a rich source of energy, key components of cell membranes and signaling molecules, and as myelin, they insulate neurons (nerve cells).

- o Vitamins are important in a range of biochemical reactions.

- o Minerals are important in maintaining ionic balances and many biochemical reactions.

- o Water is crucial to life. Metabolic reactions occur in an aqueous environment and water acts as a solvent for other molecules to dissolve in.

A deficiency of any one type of nutrient can lead to disease, starvation (or dehydration in the case of water) and subsequent death. There is also an absolute requirement for some specific molecules in the diet. This is because, although the body can manufacture most of the molecules it needs, some essential molecules cannot be made by the body. These molecules are called essential nutrients, and must be supplied in the diet. Some of these, for example are lysine and methionine, which are essential amino acids. Without them, your body can go into failure. Without these components, the body cannot work efficiently. This is extremely important when on a serious exercise regimen, where there should be in increase in consumption of both carbs and proteins. Many of the fad diets eliminate or minimize certain components in a balanced diet. This can result in a significant compromising to your ability to exercise. In some cases, it can result in a complete shut-down of the body with very serious consequences.[7]

The American Academy of Otolaryngology offers what I consider a very basic, but good advice as far as diet:

- o Eat nutrient-dense foods such as whole grains, lean proteins, fruits, and vegetables.

- o Eat slowly, and wait 10-15 minutes before taking second helpings.

- o Don't eliminate everything you like from your diet. Eat those things in small amounts (pizza, candy, cookies, etc.).

- o Prepare healthy snacks that are easily available (cut carrots, apples, etc.).

- o Drink plenty of water, especially immediately before meals.

- o Enjoy a variety of foods that will provide essential nutrients.

- o Three-quarters of your lunch and dinner should be vegetables, fruits, cereals, breads, and other grain products. Snack on fruits and vegetables. Eat lots of dark green and orange vegetables. Choose whole-grain and enriched products more often.

- o Choose lower-fat dairy products, leaner meats and alternatives, and foods prepared with little or no fat. Shop for low fat (2% or less) or fat-free products such as milk, yogurt, and cottage cheese. Eat smaller portions of leaner meats, poultry, and fish; remove visible fat from meat and the skin from poultry. Limit the use of extra fat like butter, margarine, and oil. Choose more peas, beans, and lentils.

o Limit salt, caffeine, and alcohol. Minimize the consumption of salt. Cut down on added sugar such as jams, etc. Limit beverages with a high caffeine content (tea, sodas, chocolate drinks) and caffeinated coffee to two cups per day. Minimize alcohol to one to two drinks per day.

o Limit consumption of snack foods such as cookies, donuts, pies, cakes, potato chips, etc. They are high in salt, sugar, fat, and calories, and low in nutritional value.

o Eat in moderation. If you are not hungry, don't eat.[8]

As written previously, though, you will need to consider your exercise regimen when determining your diet. You will especially need more carbohydrates and protein if you are training more. Carbohydrates are the fuel that powers your exercise regime. Carbohydrates–including wholegrain pasta, rice, sweet potato and porridge–are the most important fuel for muscles, and an essential energy source for the brain and central nervous system.

Carbohydrates are stored as glycogen in the muscles and liver. These stores are small, so a regular intake of carbohydrate is necessary to keep them topped up. Low glycogen stores may result in poor performance and increase the risk of injury.

One additional point about water and dehydration: not only does the body need water to function effectively, even being slightly dehydrated lowers metabolism. A lower metabolism can lead to weight gain, and the other effects of dehydration can lead to premature aging.

Your body needs fuel, so fuel it. Make sure any diet you adopt fulfills this basic need first and foremost.

The Substitution Diet

I hesitate to call this a diet, per se, but this is a philosophy that seems to have worked for me. It may not be good for all people, but for those who want to maintain their weight, yet take in the proper nutrients needed to have an active lifestyle, it may have some relevance.

Most diets can result in weight loss, but eating only green vegetables or only meat and fat cannot be done long-term, both for health reasons and the simple fact that we crave variety. We need to be able to follow a diet as a lifestyle change in order for it to work.

What I have done is follow a process of substitution. I take out a food that is essentially not good for my overall diet, then substitute it with something just as pleasurable, but far healthier.

When I was younger, I had a banana milkshake with every meal. I made this with vanilla ice cream, milk, and bananas. While it provided some good nutrients, that milkshake was almost 400 calories and a whopping 12 grams of fat. When I got into my 30's, I noticed a slow but steady weight gain. So I shut down the milkshake and started fruit smoothies with fruit, ice, water, and honey. I liked them equally as well as a banana shake, maybe even more so when the weather was hot, and each one had from 30-60 calories and no fat. I wasn't doing *without* so much as simply having something different. I was not missing anything. This was my first substitution. I have since made many, many more.

There are so many items that you can substitute. Try honey instead of sugar. Try a crème brulee made with low fat milk instead of cream (120 calories versus 500, and the taste is almost the same). Make French fries in the oven on hot air using a tablespoon of oil to coat them instead of deep frying them. The list goes on. The point is that you can substitute more foods than I think you would imagine at first, and this becomes a lifestyle instead of a "diet." For those of us who are not in need of major weight loss, it might be a good method to maintain weight in a reasonable range, thereby eliminating the need later in life to go on a more structured (and strict) diet.

Myth: Exercise Causes Weight Gain

Over and over again, I have had people tell me that when they exercised, they gained weight. They put in an hour three times a week on a stair stepper, but after a month, they were heavier than what they weighed before. They blame this on the exercise itself.

Poppycock.

The caveat to this is that resistance training can in fact cause weight gain in that muscle tissue weighs more than fat tissue. As you add muscle mass, even when you lose fat, the scale can read a higher number. The body-fat percentage will be lower, but the total number of pounds can go up.

Ignoring that aspect of exercise, though, an exercise regimen will not cause weight gain in and of itself. It is biologically impossible. Remember: calories in versus calories out. More expenditure of calories through exercise cannot result in weight gain if all other factors remain equal. And therein lies the rub. If you increase the caloric intake, then even with exercise, a person can in fact gain weight.

There is a characteristic that is shared among most humans. We like to reward ourselves for good behavior. We go to the gym, work out, then think that since we exercised, then that piece of pecan pie is a well-deserved treat.

Think of it, though. For an average man of 175 pounds and in his 50's, a twenty-minute moderate workout on a stationary bike might burn 150 calories. Then he goes home, has a healthy meal, but as a reward, eats that piece of pecan pie. That one piece of pie just cost him 500 calories. That is 350 more calories than he burned on the bike.

The bottom line is that if you stick with a diet, no matter what that diet is, you will lose more weight if you exercise in conjunction with that diet.

When to Eat

If ever there was a controversial subject concerning diet that seemingly should have a firm scientific answer, this could be it. While most dieticians and trainers recommend a large breakfast, a good lunch, and a light dinner, with two snacks between meals, this has come under some scrutiny. Because of that, I will ignore the strictly weight loss question and look to timing and exercise.

Most trainers do agree that exercise should not commence until from one to three hours after eating. This should be heavier on the carbs and lighter on fats and proteins. Immediately or soon after exercise, there should be a snack or meal, heavier on the protein (especially after resistance training).

A study conducted at the University of Melbourne, though, contends that to get the best result from exercise with regards to weight, the exercise should be done long after eating, as in the morning after waking up and before eating breakfast. Then, after exercise, a light meal can be taken, but it should be a number of hours before a heavier meal is eaten. In their tests, subjects who followed this routine lost significantly more weight than those who performed the same level of exercise but who ate prior to that exercise. Although not proven, the theory explaining those results is that the when exercise is conducted long after the last intake of food, the body is forced to go to the fat reserves to acquire the energy required for the exercise.

On the other hand, the Mayo Clinic recommends a more classical take on eating and exercise:

1. Eat a healthy breakfast

If you exercise in the morning, get up early enough to finish breakfast at least one hour before your workout. Most of the energy you got from dinner the previous night is used up by morning, and your blood sugar might be low. If you don't eat, you might feel sluggish or lightheaded when you exercise.
If you plan to exercise within an hour after breakfast, eat a light breakfast or drink something to raise your blood sugar, such as a sports drink. Emphasize carbohydrates for maximum energy.
Good breakfast options include:

- Whole-grain cereals or bread
- Low-fat milk
- Juice
- Bananas
- Yogurt
- A waffle or pancake

And remember, if you normally have coffee in the mornings, a cup before your workout is probably OK. Also know that any time you try a food or drink for the first time before a workout, you risk an upset stomach.

2. Size matters

Be careful not to overdo it when it comes to how much you eat before exercise. The general guideline:

- **Large meals.** Eat these at least three to four hours before exercising.
- **Small meals.** Eat these two to three hours before exercising.
- **Small snacks.** Eat these an hour before exercising.
- Eating too much before you exercise can leave you feeling sluggish. Eating too little might not give you the energy to keep you feeling strong throughout your workout.

3. Snack well

Most people can eat small snacks right before and during exercise. The key is how you feel. Do what works best for you. Snacks eaten soon before exercise probably won't give you added energy, but they can help keep up your blood sugar and prevent distracting hunger pangs. Good snack options include:

- Energy bars
- Bananas or other fresh fruit
- Yogurt
- Fruit smoothies
- Whole-grain bagel or crackers
- Low-fat granola bars
- Peanut butter sandwiches
- A healthy snack is especially important if you plan a workout several hours after a meal.

4. Eat after you exercise

To help your muscles recover and to replace their glycogen stores, eat a meal that contains both protein and carbohydrates within two hours of your exercise session if possible. Good post-workout food choices include:

- Yogurt and fruit
- Peanut butter sandwich
- Low-fat chocolate milk and pretzels
- Pasta with meatballs
- Chicken with brown rice

5. Drink up

- Don't forget to drink fluids. You need adequate fluids before, during and after exercise to help prevent dehydration.
- To stay well-hydrated for exercise, the American College of Sports Medicine recommends that you:
- Drink roughly 2 to 3 cups (473 to 710 milliliters) of water during the two to three hours before your workout.
- Drink about 1/2 to 1 cup (118 to 237 milliliters) of water every 15 to 20 minutes during your workout. Adjust amounts related to your body size and the weather.
- Drink roughly 2 to 3 cups (473 to 710 milliliters) of water after your workout for every pound (0.5 kilogram) of weight you lose during the workout.
- Water is generally the best way to replace lost fluids. But if you're exercising for more than 60 minutes, use a sports drink. Sports drinks can help maintain your body's electrolyte balance and give you a bit more energy because they contain carbohydrates.
- Let experience be your guide
- Keep in mind that the duration and intensity of your activity will dictate how often and what you should eat and drink. For example, you'll need more energy from food to run a marathon than to walk around the block.[9]

Jonathan P. Brazee

When it comes to eating and exercise, everyone is different. So pay attention to how you feel during your workout and to your overall performance. Let your experience guide you on which pre- and post-exercise eating habits work best for you. Consider keeping a journal to monitor how your body reacts to meals and snacks so that you can tweak your diet for optimal performance.

From the above, there is the Mayo Clinic and the University of Melbourne both offering a different view on when to eat while in an exercise regimen. I think the last section of the Mayo Clinic view is valid: "Let experience be your guide." Try different methods, and see what works best for you. As written before, you are the final arbiter of your own body.

Supplements

Dietary supplements are a billion dollar industry. Those aimed at people who exercise are a huge chunk of that. There are literally hundreds if not thousands of supplements that promise larger muscles, more strength, better endurance, and almost anything else.

There have been many, many studies examining supplements, and as varied as the supplements are, it is not surprising that the results of these studies are all over the map. Some supplements seem to offer benefits, some offer nothing, and some even seem to be harmful. One thing is clear, though, that for healthy individuals, most of the beneficial supplements can be replaced my diet.

The following comes from the British National Health Service:

Rick Miller, clinical and sports dietitian from the BDA, has the following advice for gym-goers and bodybuilders who want to take protein supplements:

"A simple change in foods (such as Greek yoghurt in the morning with muesli and fruit, rather than plain breakfast cereal and milk) will help enhance the protein content of a meal. After you've taken this step, fill in the gaps with a reputable brand of protein supplement. Always read the label carefully, take the recommended serving size and don't be tempted to take far more than is necessary, as this is not supported by the current evidence.

"If you're unsure, ask your GP to refer you to a registered dietitian for advice. Protein supplements are not recommended for children due to the lack of research into long-term effects."

Chris Gibbons, a competitive powerlifter from Chesterfield, says there is a danger that people may mistakenly view supplements as a quick fix to achieve their goals.

"There is a tendency to think that there is a magic powder or supplement that will give you the physique of your dreams, but there is no substitute for hard work and commitment," he says.

"Building strength takes years, not weeks or months. It is an act of discipline and must be earned through commitment to hard training and a good diet."

Protein supplements for the unwell:

However, people who are ill or disabled, unable to eat properly and weaker as a result, can use protein shakes to help them get the nutrition they need.

"Flavoured protein supplements are liquid (once mixed), often rapidly digested and may have a pleasant, sweet taste due to the variety of flavours they come in," says Azmina Govindji.

"This means that they may have a role to play in meeting your protein needs when you're unwell and other protein-rich foods (such as meat) are difficult to eat or swallow."[10]

While no harm should come from reasonable use of the bulk of the legal commercially available supplements, and there can even be some benefits, this industry is largely an exercise in marketing. With a healthy, balanced diet, none of the supplements are really needed. However, they do make it easier to ensure that you are getting the proper nutrition, and if that makes it easier for you, then by all means, use them, but use them judiciously and from reputable companies.

Please note the word "legal." There are numerous illegal supplements readily available online, mostly from off-shore sites. Some of these can be deadly. DNP (2.4-Dinitrophenol), for example, which first became popular in the 1930's, has experienced a surge among bodybuilders due to its weight-loss properties. However, there have been over 60 deaths related to its use since its resurgence. If you do decide to use supplements, buy them only from reputable sources.

EXERCISE REGIMENS

As stated before, this guide is not intended to be a comprehensive encyclopedia of exercise. I will be providing some general guidance and give examples of exercise regimens; however, for more detailed information, other sources will need to be consulted.

Once again, please remember that it is a good idea to get checked out by a physician before commencing on an exercise program, especially if you are morbidly obese or have other underlying conditions.

Equipment and Gear

No one would think of getting on an NFL football field without the proper equipment. A trip to the gym is no different. While it might not require as much equipment, there are still considerations.

Shoes: the importance of good shoes is often overlooked. A poor set of shoes, though, can lead to injury.

- Know your feet. Get them measured by a podiatrist, or at minimum, at a high-end shoe store that has the proper equipment. All major shoe manufacturers make shoes for different types of feet, and whether your feet pronate or have high arches, you need to know that in order to select a shoe made for your type of foot
- Measure your feet before purchasing. Feet do change with age
- Do not rely on one pair of shoes. Shoes appropriate for weight-training are probably not appropriate for running. Stability is a must for all shoes, but other required attributes differ for different activities
- Bring your own socks to a fitting. Use the type you will use during your training.
- Try on shoes in the afternoon or evening. Your feet will swell throughout the day, so you will want to get shoes that fit you when your feet are at their largest.

- o Forget "breaking in." Shoes should fit and feel comfortable immediately.
- o Pay attention to the fit. There should be about 3/8-1/2 inch between the front of your big toe and the end of the shoe, which is about a thumb's width. The heel should fit relatively tightly; your heel should not slip out when you walk. The upper part of the shoe should be snug and secure, and not too tight anywhere. The American Academy of Orthopedic Surgeons writes that when wearing an athletic shoe, you should be able to freely wiggle all of your toes when the shoe is on.
- o Know when to get new shoes. Worn out shoes provide less stability and cushioning. Gym shoes can probably last longer, but running shoes should be changed after 300-400 miles.[11]

Weight Belt: this could be the single most important piece of equipment for lifting weights. It should be strong, with little give, and wide enough to cover the small of the back. The lower back is probably the weakest engineered part of the body considering the load it supports, and it is the most susceptible to injury. Protect it!

Lifting Gloves: although not necessary, a pair of high-quality lifting gloves can protect the hands and make lifting weights far more enjoyable.

Clothing: comfortable clothes that allow for free movement are the baseline for most exercise activities.

- o Wear shorts or running tights as a rule-of-thumb. Baggy pants can get stuck in exercise equipment in the gym and can cause a runner to trip.
- o Steer towards clothing that has wicking capability. Avoid cotton shirts as they retain sweat.

Gadgets: don't get caught up in a gadget craze. However, having written that, some gadgets are fine for specific activities. A watch that can act as a timer or lap-counter can be beneficial, as can pulse monitors and pedometers.

Jonathan P. Brazee

Resistance Training

Resistance training is anaerobic exercise, According to current scientific studies, resistance training offers the highest benefit with regards to increasing longevity. It should be a vital component of any exercise program.

Free Weights or Machines?

What is best, working with free weights or exercise machines? Most hard core trainers recommend free weights. The prime reason for this is that it forces the body to exercise with a realistic range of motion. Machines, on the other hand, channel the motion into a smooth, limited plane. Doing a bench press, for example, on a machine exercises the main intended muscle groups of the pectoralis major as well as other supporting muscles including the anterior deltoids, serratus anterior, coracobrachialis, scapulae fixers, trapezii, and the triceps. With a barbell bench, however, the bar must also be balanced, bringing in stabilizer muscles, such as your scapula and rotator cuffs, into play. Taking it further, going to a dumbbell bench, the dumbbells are not as stable as the barbell, so even more muscles are used, to include those just getting the dumbbell into position to commence the exercise.

A study done by the California State University Department of Kinesiology and published by the Journal of Strength and Conditioning Research found that the anterior and medial deltoids and the pectoralis major were more greatly engaged when performing a bench press with free weights than when using a Smith machine (a type of weight lifting machine). The researchers concluded that free weights are more useful than the Smith machine for building muscles and strength in the upper body.[12]

With that type of research results, free weights have to be the answer, right? Well, not so fast. For hardcore bodybuilders, those who are in good shape, the answer is pretty clear that free weights are superior. This guide, though, is not aimed at that target population. It is aimed at the older man who wants to get back into shape and who may not have as much experience in a gym.

For that reason, I am going against the grain in recommending weight machines for most people. There are a number of reasons for this:

- o Safety, safety, safety: with free weights, it is important to have a spotter. With weight machines, the need for a spotter is greatly diminished, and if the weights are reasonable, the lifting can be done alone.
- o Weight machines, by design, limit the plane of motion. This significantly reduces the chance to injury.
- o If you have an injury, either chronic or temporary, weight machines offer a better opportunity to isolate the injured area and exercise unaffected areas.

Of course, for a home gym, a barbell, two dumbbell bars, weight plates, and an adjustable bench are all that is needed for a full range of resistance training. To duplicate that with machines would take up quite a number of them, which is out of the range of the typical homeowner in both cost and space required to set up the machines. For most people, the use of machines necessitates access to a gym.

Free weights are a nice addition, though. At the gym, when a trainer or spotter is available, free weights give a better indication on where you are with regards to strength fitness. And having a small set of dumbbells at home, when used in conjunction with exercises such as pushups, can be a substitute workout when something gets in the way of a scheduled gym session.

What to Exercise?

Studies seem to indicate that the longevity benefits of resistance training is related to the relative amount of muscle mass and strength in a body. While bodybuilders strive for the "perfect" body as a whole, those who are exercising for health are focused a little differently. The three main target groups would be the arms, shoulders, and chest, the back, and the thighs. While the six-pack may be great in attracting a partner, it doesn't seem to have the same impact on health as a well-developed set of pecs or quads.

In addition, besides being a major muscle group, a strong back has proven to have a significant impact on over health and mobility above and beyond other benefits. The back is the major support structure of the body, and strong muscles support the spine and reduce the risk of injury.

While there is nothing wrong with wanting cut forearms or calves, and exercising them is fine, the three major groups should be the three mentioned.

The chest, shoulders, and upper arms are normally exercised with bench presses (flat, inclined, and declined), flies, curls, deltoid raises, and military presses. Thighs can be targeted with squats and leg presses. For the back, lat pull-downs, rows, deadlifts, and back extensions.

Chest, Upper Arms, Shoulders

The upper body might be the most noticeable part of the body with regards to musculature. It is not an accident that weightlifters use the phrase "curls for girls." A well-developed upper body has the visual impact, but it also has the increased heath benefits as well as quality of life. "Strength" is often directly related to upper body strength.

The major muscle groups that are usually targeted by resistance training are the deltoids, the pectorals, the trapezius, the latissimus dorsia, the triceps, and the biceps. There are other muscles in this part of the body, but they are not as prone to increasing in mass due to resistance training.

The general exercises which target the upper body include with bench presses (flat, inclined, and declined), flies, curls, deltoid raises, and military presses.

Thighs

The thighs are made up of the quadriceps, the gluts (butt) and the thigh adductors (inner thigh). Together, they make up the largest, by mass, body part, and they react well to resistance training.

The quads and gluts are powerful muscles, and they require strenuous exercise to make them stronger. Examples of these include squats, lunges, bench jumps, and step ups. The adductors are a little more difficult, but almost every gym has an inner thigh machine.

The thighs can also get good resistance training in a form or cardio training. Bicycling is a great way to build up the thighs while doing cardio training.

Back

The back isn't only one of the body's biggest and strongest body parts, it's also the most complicated in terms of being a series of interconnected muscle groups. For the purposes of this guide, I am dividing the back into its four main regions:

- the upper and outer lats,
- the lower lats,
- the middle back
- the lower back

Each area requires specific exercises to build it up. The upper and outer lats respond best to wide grip pull down exercises, such as the pullup and the bent over barbell row. If you are not able to do a pullup, then the pullup machine can be used. The lower lats, on the other hand, should be targeted with exercises such as the reverse-grip pulldown and the straight-arm lat pulldown. All of these exercises can be done on a machine lat bar or pullup machine.

The middle back responds well to one-armed dumbbell rows as well as a close-grip cable row, while the lower back is target with exercises such as a back extension and the stiff-legged deadlift. Extreme care needs to be taken with the deadlift to keep the proper form. A poor lifting form can easily result in injury.[13]

I will provide some sample workout routines in the appendix.

How Much to Lift?

As I have stress before, exercise should be in moderation. Injury is to be avoided at all cost, and excessive effort not only has no added benefit, it can also be detrimental. Not lifting enough, though, doesn't do you much good. It is called "resistance" training, so there must be some resistance.

Everyone is different, though. What is heavy for one person is light for another. Before you can begin to determine what you should be lifting, you need to find out just where you are.

So how do you know how much you should lift? What is your benchmark?

First, forget your weights. Practice with an empty bar, even with something lighter such as a broom handle, or on a machine, with no weights hooked up. Practice on form and make sure you have the form down pat. Check with the referenced websites (provided in the appendix). Have others critique you. Video yourself. Only when you are sure you have your form correct should you start putting on weight.

For beginners, most trainers recommend something in the lines of five sets of five repetitions, three sets of eight, or three sets of ten. To determine your benchmark, try each of these with just the bar, then slowly add weight. Once your tempo begins to falter or your form begins to suffer, go back to the previous weight. This is your benchmark.

Don't try to be a hero. Be as honest with yourself as possible. Your weights will go up quickly as you get in the flow of things.

You will be dealing with quite a number of different exercises, and with each one, you will be trying to determine your benchmark. Then you will be keeping track of weights as you slowly add on as you get stronger. This can be confusing, so it is a pretty good idea to get a notebook and record each set, what you lifted, how it felt.

What about this "one rep max" about which you've been hearing? There are many workout routines that give a weight amount in terms of your one rep max, such as "lift 80% of your 1RM."

Initially, forget about it. You need to exercise at least a month or two before you even consider it. First, your 1RM will increase significantly during the first month, so it is a moving target. Second, you really need to get form ingrained in your brain and kinetic memory prior to trying to determine it.

When you are ready, to find your 1RM, you simply start low, then lift one repetition of a given exercise. Add weight and repeat.

When you fail to lift the weight, the last weight that you did lift is your 1RM.

One last thing: ignore the person lifting next to you! This is not a competition. You are not there to impress the person at the next rack. Lift what is right for you and for you alone.

Cardio

Cardio training is any training that elevates the pulse rate for an extended period of time. Examples of this would be running, swimming, biking, spinning, aerobics, rowing, some types of dancing, in-line skating, and CrossFit.

All of these are good exercises, but as mentioned before, must be done in moderation! Extreme endurance athletes suffer a wide range of aliments to include a much higher risk of early death due to inflammatory responses caused by their exercise. Forty minutes per session twice a week is more than enough to reap the benefits of cardiovascular fitness.

As we age, our bones, joints, and connective tissue degrade. Our spinal discs compress. For these reasons, I do not recommend impact exercises such as running. I have run a number of marathons, and as my knees hobble me now, I wonder how much damage the thousands of miles I put in on hard, paved roads, have done. I would also not recommend spinning for the older man. Spinning is a high intensity exercise, and I just don't see how that can be done in moderation.

Outdoor activities such as biking and in-line skating can be a fun way to exercise, and when done with others, can be socially rewarding. I have been both an avid cyclist and skater during my life, and frankly, I love both. But both have a significant chance for injury. One of my high school classmates recently crashed on his bike. He is an endurance athlete who regularly competes in triathlons, and this crash kept him out of commission for quite some time. He is a superb athlete, so he has been able to come back, but you need to ask yourself if the rewards are worth the risk.

I would recommend low impact exercises, such as biking (stationary bikes) or swimming. A recumbent bicycle is an excellent way to exercise without putting a strain on the back (and without the risk of a catastrophic crash). Swimming is great as well, with the added benefit of increasing muscle mass.

Target Heart Rate

The key to cardio fitness is the sustained elevated heart rate as a result of exercise. The target heart rate is related to age. According to the American Heart Association, roughly it is 220 minus the age of the individual. This is the maximum rate that a person should reach through exercise. The target rate is from 50-85% of that maximum rate.

Age	Target HR Zone 50-85%	Average Maximum Heart Rate, 100%
20 years	100-170 beats per minute	200 beats per minute
30 years	95-162 beats per minute	190 beats per minute
35 years	93-157 beats per minute	185 beats per minute
40 years	90-153 beats per minute	180 beats per minute
45 years	88-149 beats per minute	175 beats per minute
50 years	85-145 beats per minute	170 beats per minute
55 years	83-140 beats per minute	165 beats per minute
60 years	80-136 beats per minute	160 beats per minute
65 years	78-132 beats per minute	155 beats per minute
70 years	75-128 beats per minute	150 beats per minute

This table is for a normal, basically healthy individual. However, if you are on blood pressure medications, then these numbers will skew downwards. Please consult with a physician to determine your own individual target heart rate.

The key to cardio fitness is the sustained elevated heart rate as a result of exercise. The target heart rate is related to age. According to the American Heart Association, formula to calculate the target heart rate is 220 minus the age of the individual. This is the maximum rate that a person should reach through exercise. The target rate is from 50-85% of that maximum rate.[14]

Frequency of Cardio Exercise

As noted before, in the studies with regards to longevity, the most beneficial amount of cardio was 40 minutes twice per week. However, that is not a hard and fast rule. The American Heart Association has a different recommendation. They recommend 30 minutes per day for five to seven days a week. For them, though, these 30 minutes can be broken up into three ten-minute sessions. For their purposes, that can be a walk for ten minutes.

Just as swimming is an aerobic exercise that increases strength, weight-lifting is a resistance exercise that increases cardio fitness. Particularly when circuit training, cardio is getting an excellent workout.

High-Intensity Interval Training

One of the current popular methods of cardio is high-intensity interval training (HIIT). HIIT is a cardiorespiratory training technique that alternates brief speed and recovery intervals to increase the overall intensity of your workout.

Most endurance workouts, such as walking, running, or stair-climbing, are performed at a moderate intensity, or an exertion level of 5-6 on a scale of 0-10. High-intensity intervals are done at an exertion level of 7 or higher, and are typically sustained for 30 seconds to 3 minutes, although they can be as short as 8-10 seconds or as long as 5 minutes; the higher the intensity, the shorter the speed interval. Recovery intervals are equal to or longer than the speed intervals.

High-intensity interval training is done at a submaximal level of around 80-95% of maximal aerobic capacity. Sprint interval training (SIT) is a type of high-intensity interval training that pushes beyond this level to 100% or more of maximal aerobic capacity, or an exertion level of 10.[15]

There are advantages to HIIT-type training:

- o Significantly increased aerobic and anaerobic fitness
- o Decreased fasting insulin and increased insulin sensitivity
- o Overall weight loss when compared to other cardio programs for the same amount of exercise time

The question on HIIT, though, is if it is safe. During some studies, completed under clinical supervision, subjects with heart disease were able to tolerate the training well. However, even the proponents warn that HIIT should not be conducted more than once or twice a week in order to reduce the risk of injury. Any high-intensity exercise brings that increased risk of injury as well as an increased risk of cardiac events, so just as with spinning, it might be better to avoid this type of cardio for older men and men just starting to get back into shape.

Which Cardio Machine is Better?

Every gym has a plethora of machines. There are recumbent bikes, stair steppers, gliders, treadmills, elliptical machines, upright bikes, and so on. So with all those machines, which one is best?

The short answer is none. And all of them. As far as cardio fitness, they all are basically equal. They get the heart rate up for an extended period of time. That is their purpose.

They are different though, in how they do that. A stair stepper raises the heart rate, but it also builds up muscle in the thighs. A rowing machine also builds up the back muscles. So in order to pick the best machine for you, it comes down to two things:

- o   Aside from cardio, what other advantages do you want from it?
- o   What is more enjoyable for you to do? (If you enjoy it, you might use it more often).

Of course, the question on what is more enjoyable is somewhat dependent on the brand and model of the machine, not just the type. I rather like the recumbent bikes at one gym I use where the screen can show a virtual reality. I am sitting in a gym, but the screen shows a lake or mountain trail on which I am supposedly cycling. I also like machines where statistics are constantly being shown.

My wife, on the other hand, likes machines based on how many calories they say she is burning. The fact that the machines are notoriously inaccurate in that does not matter. She realizes that but still prefers to use the more generous machine.

(On that point, you can forget the validity of the machines which show a "fat burning zone." There is zero scientific backing for those claims.)

The bottom line is that the "best" machine is one you will use.

OTHER FORMS OF EXERCISE

The world of exercise is not limited to Resistance-training or Cardio or even how those are done. I will briefly mention some of the more established types here.

Pool Workouts

This is not swimming laps but rather doing aerobic and anaerobic-type exercises while standing in water. Working out in the pool is essentially cardio training, but done while standing in a pool. The perception is that this is exclusively for the elderly, but in fact, it is a good method for cardio while decreasing the risk of injury. It is commonly used in the horse racing industry as a way to improve stamina while limiting wear and tear on a horse, and with the value of some of those horses, if it is good enough for a California Chrome, it is good enough for a person, too.

Simply jogging in the water can be a great workout. The water forms resistance to the motion, yet buoys the body weight. In just five minutes, you can enjoy the benefits of a longer jog while significantly decrease the stress on knees and ankles.

Curls can be done under the water as well, although to be honest, just curling a heavier weight on dry land would have the same effect. The water buoys up some of the weight of the dumbbell, but the resistance of the water makes curling it a bit more difficult.

Dips can be done at the corners of the pool. Whereas most people are limited in the number of dips that they can do at a gym, that number increases when the body starts in the water and is raised out with each rise. The advantage to this is that you can smoothly do the entire exercise without jerking, getting more out of it while decreasing the risk of injury.

The same thing can be done with pushups in the shallow are of the pool. You will be able to do more pushups with your lower body in the water and your hand on the pool's edge, and your back will be a little better supported.

Flexibility exercises might actually be better in a pool as the body goes through the motions without the stress of so much weight.

Basically, your exercises in the pool are only limited by your imagination.

Yoga

While Yoga does employ the body's stabilizer muscles, it does not really impact longevity in the same way as resistance-training has been shown to do. What Yoga does, however, is reduce stress, increase flexibility, and increase balance. All of these are beneficial. Stress reduction will also increase longevity, and increased flexibility and balance will lead to a better quality of life.

I would not recommend substituting one day of resistance or cardio training, but I would certainly recommend adding another day to your schedule for Yoga.

Tai Chi

Like Yoga, Tai Chi has a place in any exercise regimen. Originally developed as a martial art, it has evolved into a form that emphasizes relaxation with slow, smooth movements. There are five schools of Tai Chi, but all spring from a standard philosophy. While the claims are that Tai Chi increases longevity, scientific studies show that it probably improves balance and general psychological health and provides general health benefits in older people. It might exercise the stabilizer muscles better than Yoga, but it falls in the same level overall, in my opinion. It is a good addition, but it should not take the place of a resistance or cardio training session.

Pilates

Unlike Yoga and Tai Chi, Pilates was developed in the 20th century by the German Joseph Pilates. It has become a popular exercise regimen, especially in the United States. Pilates centers on six principles: concentration, control, center, flow, precision, and breathing. When practiced correctly and consistently, it is designed to improve flexibility, build strength, and develop control and endurance in the whole human body. It puts emphasis on alignment, breathing, and developing a strong "Powerhouse," the body's core, and improves coordination and balance.

As with Yoga and Tai Chi, Pilates can be beneficial as a supplement to resistance and cardio, but it should not be a substitute.

CONCLUSION

There is no doubt within the scientific community that exercise—in particular, resistance training—increases life span. The numbers are very clear on this. Not only does it increase longevity, though; it improves the quality of life, it imparts a "fitness" level where older people are more capable of everyday tasks, and it has a positive impact on mental functions.

It is probably best if people adopt an exercise regimen at an early age as part of his or her lifestyle, but it is never too late. Elderly subjects enjoyed measurable benefits in as little as six weeks of exercise.

The key to exercise, though, seems to be moderation. There has yet to be results in any study that indicate strenuous exercise imparts any more longevity benefits than moderate exercise. The fact of the matter is that studies show the opposite with regards to endurance athletes; they actually have a shorter life span than the population at large.

Another point to keep in mind is that we are all aging. Father Time will not be denied. As we get older, we are more susceptible to injury, and once injured, it takes much longer to heal than when we were younger. It is imperative that in any exercise regimen, safety be a paramount consideration. Luckily, moderation in exercise is the goal, so it is easier to exercise properly with this in mind. Exercise within yourself, and listen to your body. If you feel pain, your body is telling you to stop. Don't be a "man," stubborn and prideful. Just stop what you are doing. Missing the rest of one workout is far better than missing a few months.

Don't let age, weight, injuries, "not enough time," or any other excuse keep you from starting. Exercise is one of the greatest gifts you can give not only yourself, but to your loved ones who want to have you around longer, healthy and happy.

APPENDICES

Appendix 1: Sample Exercise Routines

These are not hard and fast recommended routines. These are just samples that might be appropriate for some men. Each routine needs to be tailored to the exercises that can be done with regards to the wear and tear as well as well as an injuries suffered over the years.

Before doing any of these, please consult a trainer at best, but at a minimum, consult the images on the machines or as posted on the walls of the gym for proper form.

Routine 1: Beginner

Day 1		
Exercise	**Sets**	**Repetitions**
Leg Press	3	10
Benchpress	3	12
Row	3	10
Pullover	3	10
Squat	3	8
Lateral Side Raises	3	12
Curl	3	10
Glider or Ski Machine	1	20 Minutes
These exercises may be done with a machine or free weights. If with free weights, please use a spotter. Initially, lift three sets of each exercise. After you start feeling better, go to four sets with the same		

weight load before starting to increase the weight for each exercise.

Day 2		
Exercise	**Sets**	**Repetitions**
Leg Lift	3	10
Incline Bench	3	12
Lat Pulldown	3	10
Lateral Front Raises	3	10
Dumbbell Lunges	3	15
Fly	3	12
Curl	3	10
Recumbent Bicycle	1	20 minutes

These exercises may be done with a machine or free weights. If with free weights, please use a spotter. Initially, lift three sets of each exercise. After you start feeling better, go to four sets with the same weight load before starting to increase the weight for each exercise.

Routine 2: Intermediate

Day 1		
Exercise	**Sets**	**Repetitions**
Squat	4	10

Flat Benchpress	4	12
Inclined Benchpress	4	12
Declined Benchpress	4	12
Lat Pulldown	4	8
Lat Front Raises	4	12
Lat Front Raises	4	10
Military Press	4	10
Curls	4	10
Plank	3	One Minute
Glider or Ski Machine	1	30 Minutes

These exercises may be done with a machine or free weights. If with free weights, please use a spotter. Initially, lift three sets of each exercise. After you start feeling better, go to four sets with the same weight load before starting to increase the weight for each exercise.

Day 2		
Exercise	**Sets**	**Repetitions**
Dumbbell Lunges	4	10
Flat Benchpress	4	12
Triceps Benchpress	4	12

Jonathan P. Brazee

Row	4	12
Deadlift	4	8
Lat Front Raises	4	12
Lat Side Raises	4	10
Military Press	4	10
Curls	4	10
Plank	3	One Minute
Glider or Ski Machine	1	30 Minutes

These exercises may be done with a machine or free weights. If with free weights, please use a spotter. Initially, lift three sets of each exercise. After you start feeling better, go to four sets with the same weight load before starting to increase the weight for each exercise.

Routine 3: Working for One Repetition Max (1RM)

As noted earlier, I almost hesitate to include this, but on the other hand, it gives a good mental goal that helps keep up the discipline to exercise.

The below is set up for a 1RM on the bench press. However, the same theory is good for the 1RM for any set exercise.

There are two keys: the progressing of heavier weights, and then the associated exercises. The progression is pretty obvious. The associated exercises are exercises that work out minor muscles that help with the lift or exercises that affect muscles in a slightly different manner. In the example below, the major muscles used in the bench press are the muscles of the chest. However, strong triceps are also needed for a maximum lift, so the triceps press addresses this. A

52

straight bench works the middle chest, to the incline and declined are added to increase the upper and lower chest.

This exercise "insert" is done in the place of the main exercise, in this case, the bench press. After completion, continue with your normal routine.

Flat Bench Press 1CR Routine			
Exercise	**Sets**	**Repetitions**	**Comments**
Bench Press	4	8	Find out what weight you can comfortably lift for four sets of eight. You should be fatigued, but there should be no break in form.
Bench Press	1	5	Add weight. As a guide, if your baseline is below 175 pounds, then add in five pound increments. If it is 175 lbs or more, add in ten pound increments. Adjust the increments as needed.
Bench Press	1	4	Add another increment
Bench Press	1	3	Add another increment
Bench Press	1	2	Add another

			increment
Bench Press	1	1	Add another increment
Inclined Bench	4	8	75% of bench baseline
Declined Bench	4	8	75% of bench baseline
Triceps Bench (narrow grip bench press)	4	10	50% of bench baseline
Adjust the inclined, declined and triceps benches as appropriate. Once again, you should be fatigued, but the weight should light enough so that form is never lost.			

Appendix 2: Images

These images are for some of the exercises describe while using free weights. For machines, please see the images and instructions on each machine.

Bench Press Grips (thumb outside)	
Base distance for normal grip. Forearms need to be at a 90 degree angle to floor.	Normal grip, full extension

Wide grip (better workload for chest)	Narrow grip (tricep press)

Shoulder Exercises	
	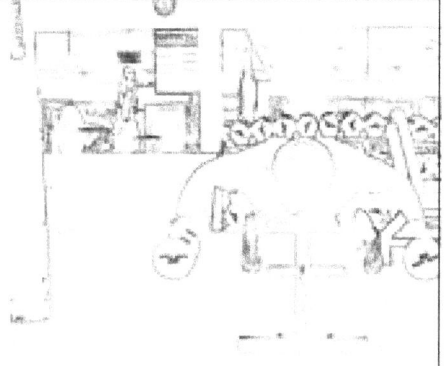
Supported Rear Lateral Raise	Extension

Front Lateral Raise	Complete with both arms.

Side Lateral Raise

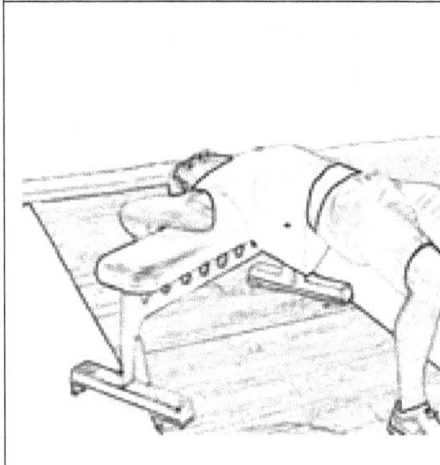

Dumbbell Pullover

Back	

Deadlift	

Squat	

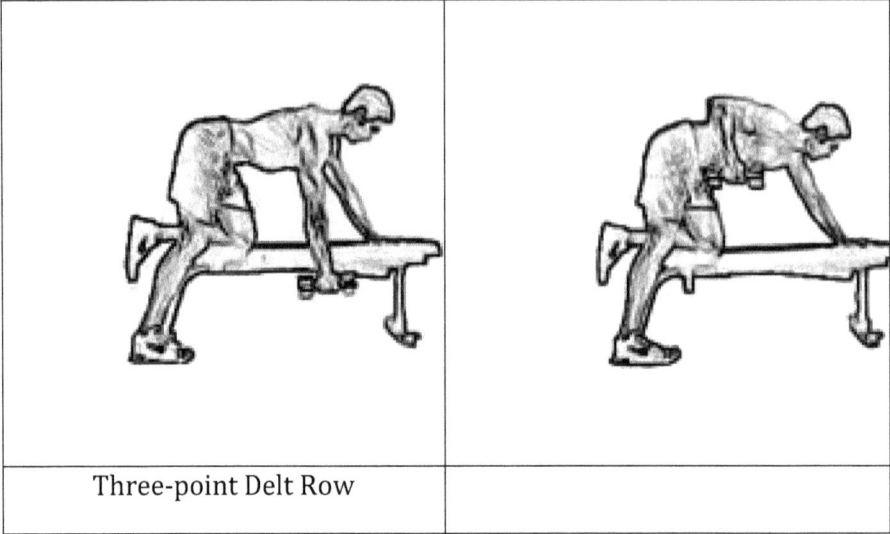

Three-point Delt Row

Appendix 3: Sample Workout Notes

Jul 13, 2014 1:15 PM Miller's Gym Routine 1	
Condition	Feel a bit lazy. Out too late last night and no energy. Hard to get going. Ate breakfast but no lunch yet.
Leg press	4 sets, 10 reps. 200 lbs. No issue, went up fine
Flat bench	4 sets, 12 reps. 125 lbs. Easy peasy. Great form. I think I am ready to move up.
Row	4 sets, 10 reps 90 lbs. This still is a little hard. I think I am jerking too much.
Pullover	4 sets, 10 reps 80 lbs Felt a twinge on third set, so quit. Feel OK for more, though.
Squat	4 sets, 10 reps 100 lbs Tried it with dumbbells and it is much harder than on the machine
Deltoid raises	4 sets, 10 reps 20 lbs Still hard to maintain form. Go down to 15 lbs?
Curl	4 sets, 10 reps, 20 lbs Curls for girls! Went great. Watched in mirror and had great form
Glider	30 minutes Put on level 6. Breathing hard after five minutes, but still not bad.

There is no real form for notes. They are for your benefit, although if you have a trainer, he or she should be able to understand your writing and what you mean. The key is to keep an accurate track of how you felt and what you did. That is the only way to know what is happening to you.

ABOUT THE AUTHOR

Jonathan Brazee is a retired Marine colonel who splits his time between North Las Vegas and Bangkok due to his work. He attended the US Naval Academy, the University of California, San Diego, and the United States International University, earning bachelor, masters, and doctoral degrees.

A decent athlete, Jonathan has spent most of his life in competitive sports, earning national championships in rugby and equestrian events. He was an avid biker and acceptable runner, with a personal marathon best of 3:06:26. After getting injured in Iraq, though, his days on the fields of competition were essentially over, and he had to come up with a better way to stay fit. Although he did weight training as part of sports fitness, he was far from a gym rat. It was the rehabilitation he went through with the military that formed the foundation of his current exercise regimen, buttressed and adjusted as a result of his in-depth research how to best maximize the benefits of exercise.

Entering the new phase of his active life, he quickly put on about 10 pounds but lowered his body fat by 4%. After seeing the plaques on the wall of Miramar Marine Corps Air Station gym for the "300 Pound Club," he had a new goal, and within six months, was able join the club with a 300-pound bench press at the age of 54. Since then, he has achieved a 1RM of 315 pounds at 56 years of age. This was achieved despite the lingering effects of losing part of his shoulder and other injuries (he is unable to perform an incline press or military press at all, for example due to his shoulder).

Jonathan has published numerous academic and other non-fiction over the years, winning one national writing award. Other than one short story, he stayed away from writing fiction, something close to his heart. It wasn't until 2009 that he wrote his first fiction novel, *The Few*. Since then, he has achieved moderate success with military, paranormal, and science fiction novels.

This guide is a result of encouragement from two of the men who have taken advice from him in order to get back into shape. Jonathan is *not* a certified fitness counselor, but his own experience and success, coupled with his deep research into the subject, form the basis for him to be able to offer others a summary of current science on exercise and longevity as well as his advice to others on exercise.

The author with name on plaque for Miramar Marine Air Station's 300 LB Club. Age: 53 years, 343 days.

ENDNOTES

1. http://www.senescence.info/ (back)
2. http://io9.com/5953154/why-getting-physically-stronger-will-help-you-to-live-longer (back)
3. Schnohr, Peter, Jacob Marott, Peter Lange, Gorm Jensen, "Longevity in Male and Female Joggers: The Copenhagen City Heart Study," American Journal of Epidemiology, February 28, 2013. (back)
4. http://fitness.mercola.com/sites/fitness/archive/2012/12/21/extreme-endurance-cardio.aspx (back)
5. Newman AB., Kupelian V, Visser M., Simonsick EM., Goodpaster BH., Kritchevsky SB., et al. "Strength, but not muscle mass, is associated with mortality in the health, aging and body composition study cohort." Journal of Gerontology, 2006;61: 72-7. (back)
6. http://oldschoolnewbody.com/5steps/ (back)
7. http://labspace.open.ac.uk/mod/oucontent/view.php?id=474957&section=1.1.1 (back)
8. https://www.entnet.org/content/diet-and-exercise-tips (back)
9. http://www.mayoclinic.org/healthy-living/fitness/in-depth/exercise/art-20045506 (back)
10. http://www.nhs.uk/Livewell/Pharmacy/Pages/Body-building-and-sports-supplements-the-dangers.aspx (back)
11. http://www.webmd.com/fitness-exercise/features/how-choose-athletic-shoes?page=2 (back)
12. http://www.livestrong.com/article/76123-difference-between-bench-press-weights/ (back)
13. http://www.muscleandfitness.com/workouts/back-exercises/back-exercises-complete-back-workout (back)
14. http://www.heart.org/HEARTORG/GettingHealthy/PhysicalActivity/Target-Heart-Rates_UCM_434341_Article.jsp (back)
15. http://www.acefitness.org/acefit/fitness-fact-article/3317/high-intensity-interval-training/ (back)

BIBLIOGRAPHY

American Academy of Otolaryngology, Diet and Exercise Tips, from www.entnet.org.

Bacon, C. G., Mittleman, M. A., & Kawachi, I. Sexual function in men older than 50 years of age: Results from the health professionals follow-up study. Annals of Internal Medicine, 139, 161-168. 2003.

Bortz, W. M. 2nd, & Wallace, D. H. Physical fitness, aging, and sexuality. Western Journal of Medicine, 170, 167-175. 1999.

Blair SN, Kohl HW 3rd, Barlow CE, Paffenbarger RS Jr, Gibbons LW, Macera CA. Changes in physical fitness and all-cause mortality. A prospective study of healthy and unhealthy men. JAMA, 1995;273:1093-8.

Blair SN, Kampert JB, Kohl HW 3rd, Barlow CE, Macera CA, Paffenbarger RS Jr, et al. Influences of cardiorespiratory fitness and other precursors on cardiovascular disease and all-cause mortality in men and women.JAMA1996;276:205-10.

Blair SN, Kohl HW 3rd, Paffenbarger RS Jr, Clark DG, Cooper KH, Gibbons LW. Physical fitness and all-cause mortality. A prospective study of healthy men and women. JAMA 1989;262:2395-401.

Calle EE, Thun MJ, Petrelli JM, Rodriguez C, Heath CW Jr. Body-mass index and mortality in a prospective cohort of US adults. N Engl J Med1999;341:1097-105.

Cooper, Rachel, Kuh, Diana, hardy, Rebecca., Objectively measured physical capability levels and mortality: systematic review and meta-analysis, [1]MRC Unit for Lifelong Health and Ageing and Division of Population Health, University College London, London WC1B 5JU.

Dvorsky, George. Why Getting Physically Stronger Will Help You Live Longer. From io90.com.

Ekelund LG, Haskell WL, Johnson JL, Whaley FS, Criqui MH, Sheps DS. Physical fitness as a predictor of cardiovascular mortality in asymptomatic North American men. The lipid research clinics mortality follow-up study. New England Journal of Medicine, 1988;319:1379-84.

Finch, C. E. (1976). "The regulation of physiological changes during mammalian aging." Q Rev Biol 51(1):49-83.

Fit Facts, from acefitness.com.

FitzGerald SJ, Barlow CE, Kampert JB, Morrow JR, Jackson AW, Blair SN. Muscular fitness and all-cause mortality: prospective observations. J Phys Act Health2004;1:7-18.

Franceschi, C., Bonafe, M., Valensin, S., Olivieri, F., De Luca, M., Ottaviani, E., and De Benedictis, G. (2000). "Inflamm-aging. An evolutionary perspective on immunosenescence." Ann N Y Acad Sci 908:244-254

Frauman, D. C. (1982). The relationship between physical exercise, sexual activity, and desire for sexually activity. The Journal of Sex Research, 18, 41-46.

Gale CR, Martyn CN, Cooper C, Sayer AA. Grip strength, body composition, and mortality. Internatioanl Journal ofEpidemiology, 2007;36:228-35.

Haavio-Mannila, E., & Purhonen, S. (2001). Slimness and self-rated sexual attractiveness: Comparisons of men and women in two cultures. Journal of Sex Research, 38, 102-111.

Holman, Steve, 5 Steps to Looking 10 Years Younger, from oldschoolnewbody.com.

Hughes VA, Frontera WR, Wood M, Evans WJ, Dallal GE, Roubenoff R, et al. Longitudinal muscle strength changes in older adults: influence of muscle mass, physical activity, and health. J Gerontol A Biol Sci Med Sci2001;56:B209-17.

Katzmarzyk PT, Craig CL. Musculoskeletal fitness and risk of mortality. Med Sci Sports Exercise, 2002;34:740-4.

Krucoff, C., & Krucoff, M. (2000). Peak performance. American Fitness, 19, 32-36.

Laukkanen P, Heikkinen E, Kauppinen M. Muscle strength and mobility as predictors of survival in 75-84-year-old people. Age Ageing, 1995;24:468-73.

Lee, M. S.; Ernst, E. (2011). "Systematic reviews of t'ai chi: An overview". British Journal of Sports Medicine 46 (10): 713–. doi:10.1136/bjsm.2010.080622.

Lee CD, Blair SN, Jackson AS. Cardiorespiratory fitness, body composition, and all-cause and cardiovascular disease mortality in men. American Journal Clinical Nutrition, 1999;69:373-80.
Magalhaes, Joao Pedro de, Senescence, from senescence.info.

Mercola, Extreme Endurance Cardio May Do More Harm than Good, from mercola.com.

Metter EJ, Talbot LA, Schrager M, Conwit R. Skeletal muscle strength as a predictor of all-cause mortality in healthy men. J Gerontol A Biol Sci Med Science, 2002;57:B359-65.

Mora S, Redberg RF, Cui Y, Whiteman MK, Flaws JA, Sharrett AR, et al. Ability of exercise testing to predict cardiovascular and all-cause death in asymptomatic women: a 20-year follow-up of the lipid research clinics prevalence study. JAMA 2003;290:1600-7

Myers J, Prakash M, Froelicher V., Do D, Partington S., Atwood JE. Exercise capacity and mortality among men referred for exercise testing. New England Journal of Medicine, 2002;346:793-801.

Nagamatsu, Lindsay S. MA; Todd C. Handy, PhD; C. Liang Hsu, BSc; Michelle Voss, PhD; Teresa Liu-Ambrose, PT, PhD. Resistance Training Promotes Cognitive and Functional Brain Plasticity in Seniors With Probable Mild Cognitive Impairment. Arch Intern Med. 2012;172(8):666-668. doi:10.1001/archinternmed.2012.379.

Newman AB, Kupelian V, Visser M, Simonsick EM, Goodpaster BH, Kritchevsky SB, et al. Strength, but not muscle mass, is associated with mortality in the health, aging and body composition study cohort. J Gerontol A Biol Sci Med Science, 2006;61:72-7.

Partridge, L., and Mangel, M. (1999). "Messages from mortality: the evolution of death rates in the old." Trends in Ecology and Evolution 14(11):438-442.

Phillips P., Grip strength, mental performance and nutritional status as indicators of mortality risk among female geriatric patients. Age Ageing, 1986;15:53-6.

Pollock ML, Franklin BA, Balady GJ, Chaitman BL, Fleg JL, Fletcher B, et al. AHA science advisory. Resistance exercise in individuals with and *without cardiovascular disease: benefits, rationale, safety, and prescription: An advisory from the Committee on Exercise, Rehabilitation, and Prevention, Council on Clinical Cardiology, American Heart Association; position paper endorsed by the American College of Sports Medicine. Circulation 2000;101:828-33.*

Rantanen T, Harris T, Leveille SG, Visser M, Foley D, Masaki K, et al. Muscle strength and body mass index as long-term predictors of mortality in initially healthy men. J Gerontol A Biol Sci Med Science, 2000;55:M168-73.

Russell, W. R., & Cox, R. H. Social physique anxiety, body dissatisfaction and self-esteem in college females of differing exercise frequency, perceived weight discrepancy, and race. Journal of Sport Behavior, 26, 298-319. 2002.

Sasaki H, Kasagi F, Yamada M, Fujita S. Grip strength predicts cause-specific mortality in middle-aged and elderly persons. American Journal of Medicine, 2007;120:337-42.

Schnohr, Peter, Jacob Marott, Peter Lange, Gorm Jensen, "Longevity in Male and Female Joggers: The Copenhagen City Heart Study," American Journal of Epidemiology, February 28, 2013.

Stump CS, Henriksen EJ, Wei Y, Sowers JR. The metabolic syndrome: role of skeletal muscle metabolism. Ann Med 2006;38:389-402

Sui X, LaMonte MJ, Laditka JN, Hardin JW, Chase N, Hooker SP, et al. Cardiorespiratory fitness and adiposity as mortality predictors in older adults. JAMA 2007;298:2507-16.

Sui X, LaMonte MJ, Blair SN. Cardiorespiratory fitness as a predictor of nonfatal cardiovascular events in asymptomatic women and men. Am J Epidemiology, 2007;165:1413-23.

Sui X, LaMonte MJ, Blair SN. Cardiorespiratory fitness and risk of nonfatal cardiovascular disease in women and men with hypertension. Am J Hypertension, 2007;20:608-15.

Swallow EB, Reyes D, Hopkinson NS, Man WD, Porcher R, Cetti EJ, et al. Quadriceps strength predicts mortality in patients with moderate to severe chronic obstructive pulmonary disease. Thorax, 2007;62:115-20.

Wiederman, M. W., & Hurst, S. R. (1998). Body size, physical attractiveness, and body image among young adult women: Relationships to sexual experience and sexual esteem. The Journal of Sex Research, 35, 272-281.

Williams MA, Haskell WL, Ades PA, Amsterdam EA, Bittner V, Franklin BA, et al. Resistance exercise in individuals with and without cardiovascular disease: 2007 update: a scientific statement from the American Heart Association Council on Clinical Cardiology and Council on Nutrition, Physical Activity, and Metabolism. Circulation 2007;116:572-84.

Wilmore, J., Knuttgen, H. 2003. Aerobic Exercise and Endurance Improving Fitness for Health Benefits. The Physician and Sportsmedicine, 31(5). 45. Retrieved October 5, 2006, from ProQuest database.

Wolfe RR. The underappreciated role of muscle in health and disease. American Journal of Clinical Nutrition 2006;84:475-82.

Other books by Jonathan Brazee

Fiction
The Return of the Marines Trilogy

The Few
The Proud
The Marines

The Al Anbar Chronicles: First Marine Expeditionary Force--Iraq

Prisoner of Fallujah
Combat Corpsman
Sniper

The United Federation Marine Corps
Recruit
Sergeant
Lieutenant (coming soon)

To The Shores of Tripoli

Werewolf of Marines
Semper Lycanus
Book 2 (Dec 2014)

Wererat

Darwin's Quest: The Search for the Ultimate Survivor

Non-Fiction

Author Website

http://www.returnofthemarines.com

www.ingramcontent.com/pod-product-compliance
Lightning Source LLC
Chambersburg PA
CBHW060658030426
42337CB00017B/2681